FIGHTING JETS

Beekman House

Manufactured in Yugoslavia
h g f e d c b a

ISBN: 0-517-02736-4

This edition published by Beekman House, Distributed by Crown
Publishers, Inc., 225 Park Avenue South, New York, New York 10003

Library of Congress Catalog Card Number: 90-60059

Picture Credits
Arms Communications: 11; **Regis Bossu/Sygma:** 30 (bottom); **Robert
Genat/Arms Communications:** 2-3; **International Defense Images:**
56-57, 75; **R. Jolly/Arms Communications:** 14-15; **Gary Kieffer/
International Defense Images:** 65; **Kulik Photographic/DOD/MGA:**
8-9, 16, 18-19, 25 (top), 28-29, 30 (top), 39, 44, 46-47, 52, 72, 76-77, 78-79,
88; **Frank Mormillo/International Defense Images:** Cover Flap, 10,
36-37, 45, 50-51, 92-93; **Photri:** Front Cover, 12-13, 15, 17, 20-21, 22-23,
25 (bottom), 31, 32-33, 34-35, 38, 42-43, 48-49, 54-55, 61, 62-63, 64-65, 66
(bottom), 67, 68-69, 70-71, 74, 80-81, 82, 83, 86-87, 89; **Mi Seitelman/
International Defense Images:** 4-5, 6-7, 60, 66 (top), 72-73, 84-85, 95;
Frederick Sutter: 40-41, 96; **Sygma:** 53; **United States Department of
Defense:** Back Cover, 26-27, 58-59, 76, 94; **Agostino Von Hassell/Arms
Communications:** 90-91

*To extend its range, a fighter can be
refueled in flight. Here an F-14 Tomcat fills
its tanks from a special version of the
Intruder designed as a tanker. Front cover:
F-16 Fighting Falcon. Back cover: Four
F-16s in formation.*

CONTENTS

TAKEOFF

America's defensive power takes many forms—troops and armor on land, of course, and huge fleets on and beneath the oceans. There is even a defensive plan of missiles to guard against global nuclear war. But to most people, nothing can be more exciting and awesome than our screaming, gleaming military jets.

Airplanes first went into battle in World War I, almost 75 years ago. The planes of that day were driven by propellers powered by piston engines, like the engines in automobiles today. They had very little power and were made mostly of wood, wire, and cloth. Despite that, even the most traditional military person could see that warfare would be completely changed by the

presence of airplanes. Troops, and even huge battleships, could be successfully attacked by a single man flying a small airplane. Military movements could easily be seen and photographed from a bird's-eye vantage point. By World War II, a major struggle called the Battle of Britain was fought in Europe, almost completely with airplanes. Similar battles raged across the Pacific Ocean. In many cases pilots flew hundreds of miles from their bases before meeting the enemy. These air battles were called **dogfights** (words printed in boldface are explained in a section at the back of the book called the glossary) because in many ways that's just what they were like.

4

Looking more like a rocket ship than a fighter jet, the sleek F-5E Tiger II can reach speeds of over 1,000 miles per hour.

Jet power made its entrance late in the second World War in the form of a new German fighter-bomber. It was called the Me 262, and could easily outfly anything else in the skies. Today, practically every one of the more than 200 American military aircraft is jet-powered. They are either pure **turbojets** or **turbofans.**

The jet engine has proven to be one of the greatest advances in aviation history. Modern jet powerplants can turn out as much as 20 times the horsepower, per pound of engine weight, as the old-fashioned gasoline motors. Jet engines also have fewer moving parts. They work by pulling in air through an intake and greatly compressing it in a set of rapidly spinning turbine blades. The compressed air is then mixed with a fuel like kerosene and burned. As the hot exhaust blasts backward from the exhaust tube, the aircraft is pushed forward with a tremendous force called **thrust.**

Even greater thrust can be generated when jet engines are fitted with **afterburners.** These devices squirt raw fuel into the hot exhaust, and the explosion that results makes the engine twice as powerful. Any jet seen with a trail that resembles a plume of fire is said to be in "full burner." The hottest jet fighters can crank out about 40,000 horsepower with the afterburners lit.

America's air power is organized into several different

air forces, each with its own mission and equipment. The U.S. Air Force is by far the largest in total personnel and equipment. It operates tactical forces in Europe and the Far East, as well as bomber wings. It even has its own transport airline, called the Military Airlift Command. Air Force planes are also flown by Air National Guard squadrons all over the United States.

The primary goal of naval aviation is to provide safe passage on the seas. Other goals are to protect surface fleets and submarines, and to support special military missions abroad. Many Navy pilots are skilled in what is surely the most difficult "routine" feat in all flying—landing on a carrier. Imagine what it must be like to bring a hot jet fighter onto the pitching deck of an aircraft carrier. It would be hard enough in clear weather. Imagine how much more difficult in a driving thunderstorm, and at night.

The Navy's hottest carrier fighter pilots are invited to attend the Navy Fighter Weapons School, called **Top Gun.** It's a five-week "graduate school" in fighter and dogfighting tactics. Top Gun grew out of the disappointing showing by American fighter pilots in the early years of the Vietnam War. Switching from the old-fashioned tactics of years past to the hot new jet fighters with air-to-air missiles required new tactics. Many valuable dogfighting lessons had been forgotten and had to be learned all over again. Today, a Top Gun graduate is as good as any other pilot flying fighter planes anywhere in the world.

The U.S. Marine Corps is a semi-independent military assault force equipped with infantry, tanks, and even its own ships. It also has a small but very capable air force with everything from **choppers** to jet fighters. The Marines fly their own transport aircraft as well.

The Army also has a large "air force," made up mostly of thousands of helicopters. It also has a small number of fixed-wing planes.

The Army and Air Force each operate their own independent training systems. These systems crank out hundreds of new pilots every year. Naval aviation is quite different from the other services. It operates pilot-training schools at bases near the Gulf of Mexico. Marine Corps and U.S. Coast Guard pilots train alongside the Navy pilots in their early training. Later on they split off on their own.

Now we're going to take a closer look at the most awesome fighting jets in America's arsenal. Each one has a mission specialty that it can accomplish better than any other bird in the world. We'll fly with the fighters and the ground attack jets, the hottest of all aircraft. You will, as Maverick Mitchell says in the movie *Top Gun*, "Feel the need for speed!"

The durable A-4 Skyhawk first flew in 1954. It has seen heavy action in Vietnam, the Middle East, and the Falkland Islands.

FIGHTER JETS

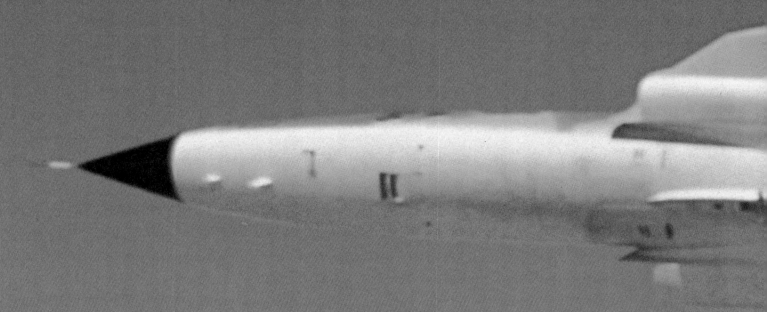

Fighter aircraft became a part of warfare over the trenches of Europe during World War I. Soon they came to be looked upon as knights of the skies, locked in lonely, furious combat with the enemy. Fighters mainly ignore the battles going on down below. Their role is to engage and destroy the aircraft of the enemy in midair. Modern American fighters are without question the most powerful in the world. In fact, most of the countries of the free world use American-made fighter jets for their own air defense.

American fighter duties are handled mainly by a group of four jet fighters. They are known as the "teen fighters" because of their designation numbers. The Navy and Marine Corps operate from both aircraft carriers and land bases. They fly the F-14 Tomcat (of the movie *Top Gun* fame) and the spectacular new F/A-18 Hornet. The F/A-18 is a dual-role fighter that can also operate as a ground-attack bomber. The Air

Force and Air National Guard fly the F-15 Eagle interceptor. They also fly the red-hot little F-16 Fighting Falcon. Hundreds of these have been put into service by the NATO countries in Europe and by other countries friendly with the United States.

Besides these newer fighters, we'll take a fond look back at the F-4 Phantom. This was the most important jet fighter of the Vietnam Era and remains a powerful airplane in the 1990s. The F-5E Tiger II is a hot but simple little fighter designed for the export market. Then there's the immense F-111 Aardvark. It is really a long-range penetration bomber that has been given an "F" designation. Normally only fighters have the letter F in their names.

So let's zip up our **G suits, check six** (in fighter talk that's directly behind our flight path, where the **bogey** usually hides), and see what jet-powered dogfighting is all about.

As viewed from below, the F-5E displays a flattened surface, unlike the otherwise rounded fuselage. Notice the deadly Sidewinder air-to-air missiles at the tips of the wings.

F-4 PHANTOM II

"Double Ugly"

The F-4G model shown above is specially equipped for "Wild Weasel" missions.

The F-4 Phantom fighter-bomber amazed the world of military aviation when it first came upon the scene. That was back in the early 1960s. When new, the haunting F-4 represented a giant leap forward in fighter design. It was far superior to anything that had gone before. It also had a battery of radar-guided and heat-seeking missiles for air combat. The Phantom became the Navy's first serious long-range interceptor. This was very important to defend a fleet of ships from attack by enemy airplanes. Later on, it evolved into a ground-attack bomber as well. The F-4 became a major player in Vietnam for the Navy, Marines, and Air Force.

The Phantom, nicknamed "Double Ugly" or "Rhino," is now nearing the end of its service with the American air forces. It remains on duty with the Air Force as an air defense fighter, attack bomber, and all-weather photo-patrol aircraft. It's still the plane of choice for the harsh and dangerous "Wild Weasel" mission. This exercise involves teasing and then attacking enemy ground-to-air missile batteries, sometimes called **SAMs.** The Weasels streak into the target area ahead of the attacking strike force. They dare the ground defenders to lock on with their search radars. If the bad guys take the bait, they'll be hit by missiles that literally fly

down the radar beam to its source. The resulting explosions cause all sorts of headaches for the enemy radar unit.

The Phantom is still big, fast, noisy, and tremendously exciting to watch in action. But it has trouble "turning and burning" with the newer teen jets in a one-on-one dogfight. And these older jets are cranky and hard to maintain in their old age. We'll see the Phantom in service for at least another decade, however, as Weasels, photo-patrol planes, and Reserve/National Guard fighters. The huge following of Phantom lovers will hate to see these wonderful airplanes fade away.

Using different kinds of camouflage colors, three Phantoms fly in formation. The one on the left is turning sharply away from the formation, or "peeling off."

You can almost feel the great power of its twin afterburning turbojet engines as this Phantom roars down the runway, about to become airborne.

The golden reflection of the low-lying sun brings out the beauty of the Phantom's design. Note the enormous fuel tanks under the wings and fuselage. Inset A study in shapes and colors as a member of the ground crew cleans the aft canopy. Just like a full-service gas station! Over 5,000 Phantoms have been built since 1958.

SPECIFICATIONS
F-4 PHANTOM II

Manufacturer	McDonnell Douglas Aircraft Company
Military Branch	Air Force, Air National Guard, Marine Corps, Navy
Type	Carrier- and land-based fighter; reconnaissance capability
Engines	Twin General Electric J79-GE-17 afterburning turbojets
Maximum speed	1,464 mph (Mach 2.2+)
Wingspan	38 ft. 5 in.
Length	63 ft. 0 in.
Height	16 ft. 6 in.
Weight	[Empty] 31,853 lbs.; [fully loaded] 61,795 lbs.
Weapons systems	Four AIM-7 Sparrow missiles; one 20-millimeter M61A-1 cannon; five weapons stations for maximum ordnance load of 12,980 lbs.
Crew	Pilot; RIO
First Flight	1958
Service entry	1960

Sporting a special paint job on the nose section, this F-4 is headed straight up—all 15+ tons of it.

F-5E Tiger II

"Little Giant"

Four of the very graceful F-5s flying in precise formation.

The beautiful little F-5E Tiger II has a slippery **fuselage,** a needle nose, and razor-thin wings. It looks awfully modern for a jet that has been around for about twenty years. Originally planned just for export to foreign countries that needed only a basic fighter, it was designed to be simple. And it is— simple to fly and simple to maintain.

No home was intended for the plane in the U.S. military inventory.

But the Pentagon bought a bunch of them anyway in the 1970s. They were destined for one special mission—to pretend to be enemy supersonic fighters (particularly the Soviet MiG-21, which they closely resemble). So the Tiger wound up in training dogfights with top Navy, Marine, and Air Force fighter **jocks.** The Air Force operates four squadrons of Tigers pretending to be "Aggressors." They're done

up in an array of Russian and Third-World camouflage paint jobs. Even their nose numbers are over-sized, just like the numbers on Russian planes. The Navy's Top Gun school uses the F-5E in the same way, but lately they're being replaced. It seems that after 15 years of dogfighting, the Navy Tigers are nearly worn out. Another teen fighter, the F-16, will soon take on the aggressor role.

An F-5 in camouflage paint, flying solo, and carrying two AIM-9 Sidewinder wingtip missiles.

USAF
015 57TH

Three of the F-5 two-seater models are seen cruising in formation. Notice the Canadian Air Force markings.

SPECIFICATIONS

F-5E TIGER II

Manufacturer	Northrop Corporation
Military branch	Air Force, Navy
Type	Tactical fighter
Engines	Twin General Electric J85-GE-21 afterburning turbojets
Maximum speed	1,083 mph (Mach 1.6+)
Wingspan	26 ft. 8 in.
Length	47 ft. 3¾ in.
Height	13 ft. 4¼ in.
Weight	[Empty] 9,683 lbs.; [fully loaded] 24,722 lbs.
Weapons systems	Two 20-millimeter M39A2 cannon; two AIM-9 missiles; ordnance load of 7,000 lbs.
Crew	Normally only the pilot, although there are two-seat versions
First flight	1969
Service entry	1972

Unusual angle from underneath an Air Force F-5. Notice the angular, flattened bottom of the fuselage and the large pylon in the center for a fuel tank or bombs.

F-14 TOMCAT

"Top Gun"

The wings on this F-14 Tomcat are in the forward position for takeoffs and landings.

The world's main air-defense interceptor is the mighty F-14 Tomcat. It is the aerial star of the movie *Top Gun* and the dreaded foe of an enemy intending to attack an American surface fleet. The Tomcat, which is based on aircraft carriers, is a twin-engine fighter with **variable-sweep wings** (wings that can be moved forward or backward in flight, or folded for easier storage aboard a carrier). It has a two-member crew: pilot up front, Radar Intercept Officer (**RIO**) —handling radar and weapons—in the back.

The Tomcat can be set up to carry six AIM-54 Phoenix air-to-air missiles. These are linked to a superradar system that can track 24 different aerial targets at the same time and launch the Phoenix missiles (or shorter-range Sparrow and Sidewinder missiles) at the most threatening **bandit.** The big jet also packs a six-barrel, 20-millimeter **Gatling-type gun** for close-range attacks. This is used in case any bogeys somehow slip past the screen of missiles.

The Tomcat is huge for a fighter. The general feeling in the fighter world is that smaller is better, because the smaller you are, the harder you are to see. And the Turkey can be seen from very far away. Despite its large size, however, it is an incredibly agile dogfighter. It can slow down and turn like crazy when the pilot motors those gigantic, variable-sweep wings into forward position. And soon all current and new Tomcats will be getting the far superior General Electric F-110 turbofan engines. These will give them the energy they've needed for world-class air combat maneuvering (ACM).

Above Cruising with wings fully forward in a sweep of 68 degrees. **Below** With its wings fully back to 20 degrees, this F-14 is ready for high-speed flight.

This is the same kind of fighter that was featured in the movie Top Gun, pictured just above the deck of a carrier.

USS AMERICA

Tomcat flying above the clouds, silhouetted by spectacular sunlight.

SPECIFICATIONS

F-14 TOMCAT

Manufacturer	Grumman Aerospace Corporation
Military branch	Navy
Type	Carrier- and land-based, multi-role fighter
Engines	Twin Pratt & Whitney TF30-P-412A or 414A afterburning turbofans
Maximum speed	1,544 mph (Mach 2.3+)
Wingspan	[68-degree sweep] 38 ft. 2½ in.; [20-degree sweep] 64 ft. 1½ in.
Length	62 ft. 8 in.
Height	16 ft. 0 in.
Weight	[Empty] 39,310 lbs.; [fully loaded] 74,348 lbs.
Weapons systems	One 20-millimeter M61A-1 cannon; various combinations of AIM-7 Sparrow, AIM-9 Sidewinder, and AIM-54 Phoenix missiles; maximum ordnance load of 14,500 lbs. of bombs or other weapons
Crew	Pilot; RIO
First flight	1970
Service entry	1974

Above From inside the cockpit, a crew member scans the horizon, on the alert for bogeys while his wingman trails alongside, off to starboard. **Below** F-14 about to touch down on the deck of the America. A carrier landing is a tricky maneuver under ideal weather conditions. In really nasty weather it can be "white-knuckle time."

F-15 EAGLE

"Foxbat Killer"

A scene from Star Wars? Two F-15s streak through—not above—a large canyon.

The F-15 Eagle is a big, bad, air defense fighter, designed for use over land rather than over the ocean. Although its size and twin vertical tails make it look a lot like the Tomcat, the F-15 is a completely different plane. Unlike the F-14, however, the F-15 has fixed (nonmovable) wings and only a pilot on board—no weapons operator.

When used for air-defense, it can carry four Sparrow radar missiles and four Sidewinder heat-seeking missiles for the close-in fight. It also carries the same type of 20-millimeter cannon that the Tomcat has. In its prime, nothing in the skies rivaled the F-15 for close-in combat, not even the Soviets' ultra-fast "Foxbat," the MiG-25 spy plane. (Thus the nickname, "Foxbat Killer.")

The F-15 has seen plenty of action in the Middle East, and has earned quite a reputation for blowing enemy planes to pieces. The Eagle was designed to be "user-friendly," and earns the highest praise from the **jockeys** who drive it.

A different version, the F-15E Strike Eagle, is a new two-seater with uprated engines. It is being set up for the deep ground-strike missions now being handled by the F-111.

An Eagle cruising above the clouds. Notice the lights on the leading edge of the wings and the fuel tank under each wing. Each tank holds about 600 gallons.

33

A trio of F-15 Eagles flying in close formation. They can reach speeds of over 1,600 miles per hour. Inset A deadly combination: The Eagle and Sparrow. This Eagle has just fired an AIM-7 Sparrow air-to-air missile. Bogeys beware!

SPECIFICATIONS
F-15 EAGLE

Manufacturer	McDonnell Douglas Aircraft Company
Military branch	Air Force, Air National Guard
Type	Fighter; attack capability
Engines	Twin Pratt & Whitney F-100-PW-100 afterburning turbofans
Maximum speed	1,650+ mph (Mach 2.5+)
Wingspan	42 ft. 9¾ in.
Length	63 ft. 9 in.
Height	18 ft. 5½ in.
Weight	[Empty] 28,600 lbs.; [fully loaded] 68,000 lbs.
Weapons systems	One 20-millimeter M61A-1 cannon; various combinations of AIM-7 Sparrow, AIM-9 Sidewinder, and AIM-54 Phoenix missiles; maximum external ordnance load of 23,600 lbs.
Crew	Normally only the pilot, although there are two-seat versions
First flight	1972
Service entry	1976

An Eagle screams.

F-16 FIGHTING FALCON

"Electric Jet"

With sunlight reflecting from its smooth fuselage, an F-16 soars.

The General Dynamics F-16 was the fighter success story of the 1970s and 1980s. It was the winner of the NATO fighter design competition in the early 1970s. In the mid-1970s it entered service with the U.S. Air Force and the air forces of several other countries. Eventually, 7,000 will be built. Perhaps 40 different countries will eventually fly them. This tiny, single-engine jet is just about the most astonishing dogfighter on the scene today. It can accelerate while flying straight up and crank out 9-**G** turns until the pilot passes out. (This can actually be a serious problem, since the plane can easily dish out more Gs than most humans can take.)

The Falcon is also designed to put in duty as an attack bomber aided by computer. Its capabilities in this area are equally impressive. The majority of Israeli F-16s are two-seaters set up as bombers with a weapons officer in the back seat.

Computerized flight controls are another hallmark of the F-16. Normally, airplane controls are operated by mechanical means. In the F-16, the surfaces that control flight work by a method called "**fly-by-wire.**" That means they are told what to do by a computer. The computer takes its directions from a small, side-stick controller on a console on the right side of the cockpit. This approach to aircraft design has earned the F-16 the nickname "**Electric Jet.**" The pilots say it all takes some getting used to, though once they've got it, look out! Other jets may have more impressive long-range weapons systems and radars, but nothing else flying can do any better in a close-in **knife fight.**

With wingtip missiles in place, this Falcon is headed north. An F-16 can actually increase its speed as it climbs vertically.

39

A formation of four Falcons with wingtip missiles in place. Inset A pilot looks off to starboard at his wingmen. The F-16's canopy was designed to give the pilot excellent visibility.

The Air Force chose the F-16 for its precision flying team, the Thunderbirds. This group of Falcons is shown flying over the pyramids in Egypt.

SPECIFICATIONS

F-16 FIGHTING FALCON

Manufacturer	General Dynamics Corporation
Military branch	Air Force, Air Force Reserve, Navy
Type	Multi-role fighter
Engine	One Pratt & Whitney F100-PW-200 afterburning turbofan
Maximum speed	1,320+ mph (Mach 2+)
Wingspan	[With missiles] 32 ft. 10 in.; [without missiles] 31 ft. 0 in.
Length	49 ft. 3 in.
Height	16 ft. 8½ in.
Weight	[Empty] 18,355 lbs.; [fully loaded] 42,300 lbs.
Weapons systems	One 20-millimeter M61A-1 cannon; wide variety of bombs and missiles for maximum external ordnance load of 12,000 lbs.
Crew	Pilot; weapons officer in some models
First flight	1974
Service entry	1979

A huge variety of weapons can be carried by the Electric Jet, from 20mm ammo to nuclear bombs. Two large bombs have just been released by this pilot.

F/A-18 HORNET

"Two-in-One"

This is the plane the Navy picked for its flying team, the Blue Angels.

Designed in the early 1970s, the McDonnell Douglas/Northrop Hornet is the current favorite of Naval and Marine Corps aviation. This mid-size jet is a true fighter/bomber. It's as good at air-to-air dogfighting as it is when attacking ground targets. The Hornet can easily engage in an air-to-air dogfight just after climbing off a target run. It's a bit better than the aging A-7 light-attack jet currently being used. Eventually it will replace the A-7, for it is a whole lot better in a dogfight.

Like the F-14 and F-15, the Hornet is a **two-holer.** This means it has two engines, a pair of General Electric F-404 turbofans. They crank out some 40,000 pounds of thrust with the afterburners lit. Like the F-16, all flight controls are computerized and fly-by-wire. It also has a full-movement control stick between the pilot's legs.

All sorts of important information is quickly and easily made available to the pilot. He must have info about navigation (where he is). He must know whether or not his

weapons are ready to fire. And he must know where the enemy is. The Hornet has a system that projects all of this onto something called a **HUD** or Head-up Display. It consists of clear glass panels, set at an angle to the pilot's line of vision so it does not obstruct his view. Information from three television/radar screens is projected directly onto these panels. With this arrangement, the Hornet pilot can fly and get into a **furball** without losing sight of such critical information.

Look out below! A diving F/A-18 has just released a deadly pair of bombs.

The rush of steam remains from the last launch as the flight deck crew prepares the next Hornet for its turn. The deck of a carrier is a very dangerous place to work

SPECIFICATIONS

F/A-18 HORNET

Manufacturer	McDonnell Douglas Aircraft Company in conjunction with Northrop Corporation
Military branch	Marine Corps, Navy
Type	Carrier- and land-based fighter and attack bomber
Engines	Twin General Electric F404-GE-400 afterburning turbofans
Maximum speed	1,188+ mph (Mach 1.8+)
Wingspan	37 ft. 6 in.
Length	56 ft. 0 in.
Height	15 ft. 3½ in.
Weight	[Empty] 23,050 lbs.; [fully loaded] fighter model 36,710 lbs., attack model 49,224 lbs.
Weapons systems	One 20-millimeter M61A-1 cannon; nine external weapon stations for missiles, bombs, and rockets, with maximum external ordnance load of 17,000 lbs.
Crew	Normally only the pilot, although there are two-seat versions
First flight	1978
Service entry	1983

A pair of Canadian Hornets cruising high above the sea.

F-111 AARDVARK

"The 'Vark"

An F-111 with wings fully forward and a hefty load of bombs.

The enormous F-111 is more than just a fighter. It's an amazing all-weather penetration bomber. The Aardvark is able to strike at long distances and very high speeds, with 15 tons of deadly bombs and missiles. In 1986, U.S. Air Force F-111s attacked Libya in a highly complicated mission. It required the crews to fly some 5,750 miles from their bases in England all the way to North Africa. They couldn't land on the way to take on fuel, so they had to be refueled in flight. It took them 14 hours of flying time before they returned to their home bases.

The F-111 started out as the all-purpose "**TFX**" fighter in the early 1960s. It was a dream plane that would be able to do practically every job from a land base or a carrier. Things didn't work out that way, of course. Efforts to make the plane do too many jobs made it far too heavy. It didn't have enough power, and was extremely complicated. The Navy eventually gave up on the Aardvark completely. That left its future to the U.S. Air Force (and the Australians, who also bought it). Today, the F-111 is used very successfully at bases in Europe and the western U.S. There is a second version called the EF-111. Also known as the Raven, this **ECM** plane goes along with the rest of a strike force to its target. But while the other planes are dropping bombs, the Raven jams the enemy's radar.

The F-111 can take off at fully loaded weights of over 100,000 pounds. This is far more than the weight of the workhorse B-17 bomber of World War II, which had four engines and a crew of eight to ten. By the way, it also means the 'Vark is fully twice as heavy as four of the other fighter jets in this book. Power is provided by the same TF-30 turbofans that drive the F-14. It features amazing variable-sweep wings, which simply means that the wings move forward and backward. With its wings cranked all the way back, the big 'Vark can easily break the sound barrier at sea level. This is a feat few jets can achieve because the air is more dense there and thus offers more resistance than at higher altitudes, where it is thinner. The plane carries a crew of two, seated side by side: pilot on the left, **bombardier/ navigator** on the right.

The Aardvark as seen from a refueling tanker. The tubelike device connects to the top of the fuselage in order to transfer fuel. This method was used in the raid on Libya.

Shown banking to the pilot's left, this F-111 is packed with bombs on wings that are swept slightly back.

SPECIFICATIONS

F-111 AARDVARK

Manufacturer	General Dynamics Corporation
Military branch	Air Force
Type	Fighter; all-weather attack bomber
Engines	Twin Pratt & Whitney JF30-P-100 afterburning turbofans
Maximum speed	1,450 mph (Mach 2.2)
Wingspan	[with wings swept back] 32 ft. 0 in.; [with wings moved forward] 63 ft. 0 in.
Length	73 ft. 6 in.
Height	17 ft. 0 in.
Weight	[Empty] 46,172 to 53,600 lbs.; [fully loaded] 114,300 to 119,000 lbs.
Weapons systems	Weapons bay for two B43 bombs or one B43 and one 20-millimeter M61A-1 cannon; three pylons under each wing for maximum ordnance load of 37,500 lbs.
Crew	Pilot; bombardier/navigator
First flight	1964
Service entry	1967

Although the afterburners greatly increase fuel use, the extra power can be helpful. The stream of flame indicates that this bird is in full burner.

ATTACK JETS

Fighter pilots always seem to get the glory. When Hollywood comes calling, the first thought is to drop a star actor into a fighter plane. Recently they picked up Tom Cruise and dropped him into the awesome F-14 Tomcat. Hollywood drives the attack pilots crazy. And with good reason: the job of the fighters is only to fly cover for the attack planes. Fighters sweep the skies clean of enemy aircraft. Meanwhile, the attack planes (or "**mud-movers**") roll in low to hit the enemy with bombs, rockets, and cannon fire. The real damage to an advancing enemy will be inflicted by attack pilots. Fighter pilots nickname them "attack pukes."

Aerial attack has come a long way since World War II. The smallest jet-powered attack aircraft of today routinely carry a tremendous load of knockout weapons. More than medium and even heavy bombers could lift with their piston engines—maybe ten times as much weight! Also, internal bomb bays are now a rarity, except in the F-111 and huge strategic bombers. Most attack jets carry their deadly payloads on **universal pylons.**

Notice the unusual alignment of wheels on this VSTOL AV-8B Harrier: two under the fuselage and two smaller ones near the wingtips.

These are fixtures located underneath the wings and the fuselage or main body of the plane. They are called "universal" because the fixtures to which the weapons attach are the same for almost all countries. A new kind of bomb helps, too. **Smart bombs** are guided by laser beams or a tiny TV camera mounted in the nose of the bomb. This makes it much easier to hit the target. There are even computerized bombing systems that work with ordinary "dumb" or unguided bombs. With a system of this kind, even **nuggets** can look good.

In this section we'll take a closer look at the current American arsenal of aerial **ground-pounders.** First come the little A-4 Skyhawk, the carrier-borne A-6 Intruder, and the chunky A-7 Corsair II. Then we'll see the supremely ugly but bad-to-the-bone A-10 Thunderbolt (that's its official name, but everyone calls it the "Warthog"). Finally there is the unusual AV-8B Harrier. It's a near-supersonic jet that can hover in place like a helicopter and land vertically. So slide into the cockpit and get ready to move some mud.

A-4 SKYHAWK
"Scooter"

A two-seat Navy A-4 flies over snow-covered mountains.

The little "Scooter" goes back more than 30 years in American military service. Currently it's being replaced on the front lines as the primary light attack jet for the U.S. Marine Corps. The Skyhawk is a single-engine, one-person attack bomber with modified **delta wings** (shaped like a triangle when seen from below). These wings are so narrow that they don't even have to be folded to fit snugly on the flight deck of a carrier. Many countries around the world still fly the 'Hawk. Israel swears by them. And in 1982, during the Falklands War, Argentina had great success with their A-4s. They caused tremendous damage by repeated attacks with 500-pound bombs against a modern British naval force.

In its declining years the Skyhawk has assumed a new and exciting job. Although the oldest of the attack planes, they now fly as "adversaries" for Navy and Marine air combat training. The Navy's Top Gun school uses six specially modified A-4Fs. They're stripped of excess weight and powered by a huge Pratt & Whitney engine. The little attack bird is thus made into a tough fighter, wickedly hot and very hard to find in the sky. The Top Gun instructors call this version of the A-4 the Mongoose. With it, they take delight in regularly embarrassing new students in their first few dogfights.

Four Marine A-4s in formation. Notice the bombs and fuel tanks. The plane was designed to be simple and to carry a big load of bombs.

Bombs away! The hump along the top of the fuselage contains instruments to aid in navigation and communication.

There is no time to waste during flight operations. As steam from the catapult swirls around them, a flight deck crew hustles to launch another Skyhawk. Inset While the ground crew gathers, a carefully positioned group of six A-4s waits on the runway between flights.

SPECIFICATIONS
A-4 SKYHAWK

Manufacturer	Douglas Aircraft Company
Military branch	Marine Corps, Navy
Type	Attack bomber
Engine	One Pratt & Whitney J52-P-8A turbojet
Maximum speed	646 mph [loaded]
Wingspan	27 ft. 6 in.
Length	41 ft. 4 in.
Height	15 ft. 0 in.
Weight	[Empty] 10,800 lbs.; [fully loaded] 24,500 lbs.
Weapons systems	Two 20-millimeter Mk 12 cannon; ordnance includes air-to-air/ surface rockets, bombs, and missiles; maximum ordnance of 10,000 lbs.
Crew	Normally only the pilot, although there are two-seat versions
First flight	1954
Service entry	1956

Top *The long tube on the pilot's right or starboard side allows the Scooter to take on fuel while in the air.* **Bottom** *A Navy A-4 gets to rest before the next flight operations begin. If stormy weather hits, all aircraft must be carefully tied to the deck.*

A-6 INTRUDER

"Heavy Hitter"

Another old workhorse: Early models of the A-6 Intruder first flew back in 1960.

There's nothing pretty or graceful about the Intruder. With its bulblike nose and long tail structure it almost looks as if it's flying backward. But it isn't. In fact, the A-6 is a very serious airplane. It functions as the aircraft carrier's heavy bomber. With a bomb load of nine tons (which is heavier than five late-model Corvettes, if you can imagine that), it is quite powerful. Those bombs can be delivered at night or during the day, in conditions of zero visibility, with awesome accuracy. It's

powered by two of the same massive engines that run the single-engine Skyhawk. A crew of two is aboard—a pilot in the left seat and a navigator/bombardier next to the pilot. This differs from most other aircraft we'll see. Usually the second person sits behind the pilot.

The new version of the Intruder, called the A-6F, is due for delivery to the fleet by the end of the 1980s. It will be the Navy's leading strike aircraft throughout the 1990s. This model will be powered

by the more powerful General Electric F-404 engines—the ones that drive the F/A-18 Hornet. Plus, the right-seater will have a number of computers and weapons systems to play with. And that doesn't even include the navigation gear. The strange hooklike device in front of the windshield, by the way, is the Intruder's in-flight refueling probe. The pilot gently places it into a basketlike device that trails down behind a big tanker aircraft. The big jet can then gas up in flight and stay aloft for a long time.

Like the A-4, the Intruder has a tube for receiving fuel while airborne. The A-6 even has a version that can be used as a tanker—to refuel other planes.

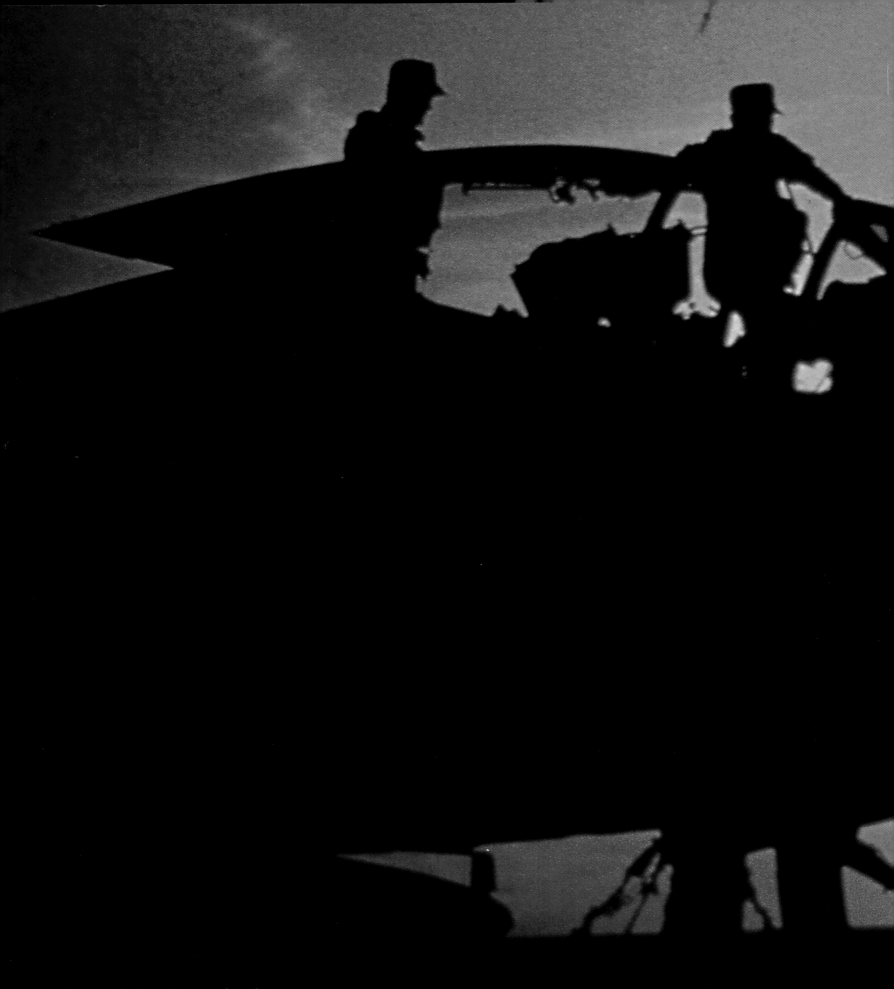

Although it looks quiet enough in this pose, the Intruder was really designed as a vehicle of destruction. Thirty 500-pound bombs pack a lot of power.

In addition to its firepower, the A-6 is noted for the fact that it can operate in all kinds of weather, even when visibility is low. *Inset* Somewhere in the Mediterranean Sea, aircraft are moved around on the hectic flight deck. The heavy wings of the A-6 are folded for easier storage.

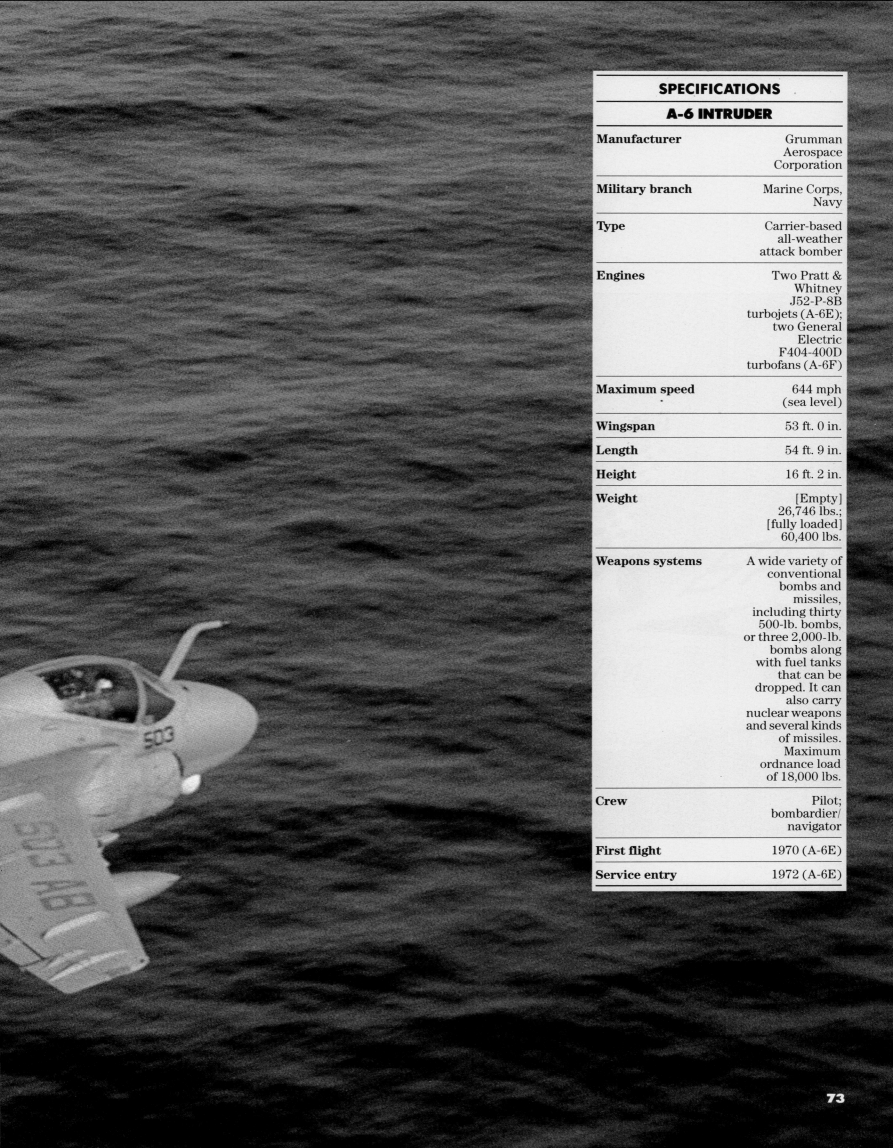

SPECIFICATIONS

A-6 INTRUDER

Manufacturer	Grumman Aerospace Corporation
Military branch	Marine Corps, Navy
Type	Carrier-based all-weather attack bomber
Engines	Two Pratt & Whitney J52-P-8B turbojets (A-6E); two General Electric F404-400D turbofans (A-6F)
Maximum speed	644 mph (sea level)
Wingspan	53 ft. 0 in.
Length	54 ft. 9 in.
Height	16 ft. 2 in.
Weight	[Empty] 26,746 lbs.; [fully loaded] 60,400 lbs.
Weapons systems	A wide variety of conventional bombs and missiles, including thirty 500-lb. bombs, or three 2,000-lb. bombs along with fuel tanks that can be dropped. It can also carry nuclear weapons and several kinds of missiles. Maximum ordnance load of 18,000 lbs.
Crew	Pilot; bombardier/navigator
First flight	1970 (A-6E)
Service entry	1972 (A-6E)

A-7 CORSAIR II

"Honored Name"

The carrier John F. Kennedy is the seaborne home for this group of A-7s.

The stubby A-7 Corsair II is manufactured by Vought Aircraft, which also made the earlier and very popular Corsair fighter/bomber. That airplane became famous during World War II.

The A-7 is a worthy successor to the honored Corsair name. It's based on a supersonic fighter of the 1950s, the F-8 Crusader—a plane that can bring tears to the eyes of older Navy jet jockeys because it was hot, sleek, and

beautiful. Many consider it the most dramatic fighter of all time. Today, the A-7 holds down the light-attack job on most Navy carriers. But it's being replaced one ship at a time by the much more powerful F/A-18 Hornet. The U.S. Air Force and several foreign air forces also operate A-7s in a variety of different models.

The single-engine Corsair has a total of eight weapons stations, six under the wings and two on the

body. These allow it to carry a deadly array of bombs, rockets, air-to-ground missiles, and electronics pods. It can also sling a pair of Sidewinder heat-seeking missiles on rails under the canopy. That's in case enemy fighters are found hanging around as the attack jets finish their bombing run. But the Corsair is definitely a bomber, not a fighter. It would be unusual for an A-7 pilot to get off a shot in a dogfight.

When flying straight up, the A-7 pilot sees little besides blue sky and the cockpit instruments.

The distinctive snub nose of the Corsair is conspicuous from this angle. Sadly, these graceful birds are being replaced with more modern attack jets. Inset This A-7 jock looks like something from another planet with the flight helmet visor in position.

406

Trailing vapor from its wingtips, this A-7 is just about to touch down on a carrier deck. The hook underneath catches a wire on deck to stop the plane quickly.

Turning together in formation, three A-7s in camouflage paint fly below the rim of a huge canyon.

SPECIFICATIONS
A-7 CORSAIR II

Manufacturer	LTV Aircraft Products Group
Military branch	Air Force, Air National Guard, Navy
Type	Carrier-based tactical attack bomber
Engine	One Pratt & Whitney TF30-6 turbofan (A); one Allison TF41-1 turbofan (D,H,K); one Allison TF41-A-2 turbofan (E)
Maximum speed	691 mph
Wingspan	38 ft. 9 in.
Length	46 ft. 1½ in.
Height	16 ft. ¾ in.
Weight	[Empty] 19,781 lbs.; [fully loaded] 42,000 lbs.
Weapons systems	One 20-millimeter M61A-1 cannon (D,E); maximum external load of 15,000 lbs. of missiles, bombs, rockets, gun pods, and fuel tanks
Crew	Normally only the pilot, although there are two-seat versions
First flight	1965
Service entry	1966

A-10 THUNDERBOLT II

"The Warthog"

The A-10 is slow, but agile and deadly, especially against enemy armor.

While the F/A-18 and F-111 are designed for two jobs, the A-10 Thunderbolt II is just the opposite. Universally nicknamed the Warthog, this oddly shaped plane is carefully designed for only one job: CAS or close air support. It is at its best when it's low, slow, and eyeball-to-eyeball with the enemy's tanks and infantry.

Although the A-10 is powered by two big turbofans, it's a slow mover, scarcely a third as fast as the teen fighters. Its huge, straight wings help it to maneuver very quickly at low speeds. As a platform for launching weapons at the enemy it is strikingly effective. The Hog is also designed to take repeated hits from ground fire and keep on truckin'. The **ejection seat** that holds the pilot is surrounded by heavy armor in the shape of a bathtub. In fact, the plane is built with as many as four independent systems. These protect flight controls and the fuel system from hostile fire. This way, if one control system is blown away, others are there to take over. By design, even the landing gear drops only halfway down.

Emergency landings can still be made despite damage to the gear mechanism.

The A-10 was designed and built around its principal armament, a 30-millimeter antitank cannon with seven rotating barrels. The big gun spews out six-inch rounds loaded with **spent uranium** that can blast through the armor of the heaviest tank. (Spent uranium is probably the heaviest metal around.) Warthogs are flown by the active Air Force in Europe and Korea, and by the Air Force Reserve in the U.S.

The wings must be very strong to carry the weight of bombs and missiles—as much as eight tons for some missions.

Basically, the A-10 was planned as a
platform for its main weapon, a monstrous
30mm cannon with seven barrels and a
devastating rate of fire. Inset This closeup
of the nose of a Warthog shows the
special paint job. More frightening by far
to the enemy is the cannon itself.

SPECIFICATIONS
A-10 THUNDERBOLT II

Manufacturer	Fairchild Republic Company
Military branch	Air Force and Air Force Reserve
Type	Close-support attack aircraft
Engines	Twin General Electric TF34-GE-100 turbofans
Maximum speed	439 mph
Wingspan	57 ft. 6 in.
Length	53 ft. 4 in.
Height	14 ft. 8 in.
Weight	[Empty] 24,959 lbs.; [fully loaded] 50,000 lbs.
Weapons systems	One GAU-8/A Avenger 30-millimeter cannon; a wide variety of bombs and missiles for maximum external ordnance load of 16,000 lbs.
Crew	Pilot
First flight	1972
Service entry	1977

Since the Warthog flies at low altitudes, the pilot gets special protection inside an armored shell. The engines are also shielded from hostile fire.

AV-8B HARRIER

"The 'Jump' Jet"

Surely the most unusual attack aircraft design is found in the Harrier.

Marine attack pilots operate the most unusual jet in the whole American military inventory—the astonishing AV-8B Harrier. It is a British-designed **VSTOL** attack craft that can actually adjust the direction of thrust of its Rolls Royce engine. This allows it to take off or land vertically. And if that weren't enough, it can also hover in flight like a big, noisy hummingbird. With this capability, the Marines have a fast ground-attack plane that is very flexible. It can operate from tiny airstrips near the battlefield or from limited flight decks on ships of relatively small size.

British and Marine Harrier pilots have also developed a special bag of dogfighting tricks that no other fighter can match. By moving the four thrust nozzles while turning the plane, the pilot can do some pretty amazing things. To begin with, he can tighten the radius of his turn in ways that are difficult for an enemy pilot to foresee. This provides a tremendous advantage in a dogfight. The nozzles can even be cranked forward to slow the little jet in level flight. A pursuing enemy plane, unable to slow down, would be forced to fly past the Harrier. The Jump Jet would then have the enemy plane directly ahead, making an easy target. With its missiles and guns, the pilot would be able to deal a knockout blow. Using similar tactics, a small number of British Harriers caused terrible damage to the Argentine Air Force in the Falklands War of 1982.

This is no ordinary airplane! Look very closely and you can see the flow of exhaust that allows this AV-8B to hover in midair like a chopper.

Although this Harrier is using a carrier's flight deck, it doesn't really need much space to land. Because of this, it can be located very near to the field of battle.

The relatively thick wings allow the
Harrier to carry heavy bombs. And the
large canopy provides great visibility,
much like that of a helicopter.

SPECIFICATIONS

AV-8B HARRIER

Manufacturer	McDonnell Douglas Aircraft Company, British Aerospace
Military branch	Marine Corps
Type	Carrier- or land-based close-support attack aircraft
Engine	One Rolls Royce Pegasus F402-RR-402 vectored-thrust turbofan
Maximum speed	662 mph
Wingspan	30 ft. 3½ in.
Length	46 ft. 4 in.
Height	11 ft. 3½ in.
Weight	[Empty] 13,086 lbs.; [fully loaded] 31,000 lbs.
Weapons systems	One 25-millimeter GAU-12/U cannon; up to nine pylons for maximum external ordnance load of 17,000 lbs.
Crew	Pilot
First flight	1978
Service entry	1983

The pilot cranks up the engines of his powerful F-14 Tomcat, waiting for the signal from the cat officer for a shot down the slippery flight deck.

GLOSSARY

Afterburner   A system that feeds raw fuel into a jet's hot exhaust, thus greatly increasing power output and fuel usage. A jet in "full burner" will burn almost ten times as much fuel as normal, so a jet pilot must control the urge to "light the pipes."

Bandit   An opponent in a dogfight that has been positively identified as an enemy or bad guy. This can happen by visual sighting or by a radio call from another jet or from the ground.

Bogey   Unidentified and possibly dangerous aircraft.

Bombardier/Navigator   All-important second crew member of the A-6 Intruder and the F-111 Aardvark.

Check six   Visual observation of the area directly behind the flight path of the aircraft, from which most air attacks can be expected. It refers generally to the clock system of scanning the area around the aircraft: 12 o'clock is straight ahead, 6 o'clock is directly behind. Also a common greeting among tactical pilots.

Chopper   A common nickname for helicopters. It probably came about because of the unusual noise made by helicopters in flight.

Delta wings   Wings that have the same shape, when seen from the ground, as the greek letter delta. In other words, the shape of an upright triangle.

Dogfight   A term from World War I that refers to the twisting and turning aerial battles between two or more fighter aircraft.

ECM   Electronic Countermeasures. A system for jamming or misleading enemy weapons, communications, or radar.

Ejection seat   In a critical situation, a powerful rocket motor will blast the pilot and his seat out of the plane. A parachute opens automatically three seconds later. Most of the aircraft in this book have ejection seats for each crew member.

Electric Jet   The F-16 Fighting Falcon has been given this nickname because of its fly-by-wire controls.

Fly-by-wire   A system of operating the control surfaces of an aircraft—like the rudder—with electronics and computers. This has replaced the older system that used mechanical and hydraulic means of control. The F-16 and F/A-18 use this new method.

Furball   A confused dogfight with many airplanes.

An A-10 Thunderbolt, better known as the Warthog, taxis toward the photographer—a menacing sight.

Fuselage   The main body of a jet aircraft. The pilot and crew are located within the fuselage section. The wings are not part of the fuselage.

G   Powerful jets—and the pilots in them—suffer a great deal of stress from the forces of gravity. It's kind of like what you feel when riding in a fast elevator, on a roller coaster, or in a passenger airplane at take off, only much worse. One "G" is equal to normal gravity, which you don't even notice. But in a sharp turn, the force is very strong. Jet pilots are said to "pull 4 Gs" when they feel four times normal gravity.

Gatling gun   Originally the rapid-fire, six-barrelled gun of the late 1860s, which was operated by a hand crank and named after its American inventor, Richard J. Gatling. Today it refers generally to the high-speed, six-barrelled guns found on many military aircraft.

G suit   A nylon outfit worn by all crew members on fast jets. It wraps around the legs and stomach area. In fast movements, called "high-G maneuvers," the G suit automatically fills with air. This helps to prevent blood from pooling in the lower part of the body. When that happens, the pilot or crew member risks the danger of blacking out.

Ground-pounder   See "mud-mover."

HUD Head-up Display. A transparent screen on the dashboard of the cockpit. Important info from different instruments is projected onto this screen. This allows the pilot to read the instruments without looking away from the windshield.

Jockey, jock Other terms for pilot.

Knife fight Low-speed dogfight at close range.

Mud-mover Attack planes that operate close to the ground. Examples are the A-6, A-7, and A-10. The F/A-18 doubles as both a fighter and "mud-mover."

Nugget Slang term for a rookie pilot.

Ordnance Refers generally to bombs, missiles, and ammunition; the weapons that fire them; and related equipment such as launching devices and the pylons to which bombs are attached.

RIO Radar Intercept Officer. The weapons and navigation expert in the back seat of the F-14 Tomcat and the F-4 Phantom. See "WIZZO."

SAM Surface-to-Air Missile. Antiaircraft missiles launched from the ground. They were often used against jets over Vietnam.

Smart bombs Bombs that are guided—by lasers or tiny TV cameras—and far more accurate than regular bombs.

Speed of heat Very, very fast.

Speed of thought Even faster than the "speed of heat." Also referred to as "Warp One."

Spent uranium A metal that is in essence nonradioactive, but is super heavy. It is an excellent material for use in armor-piercing bullets.

TFX Tactical fighter, experimental.

Thrust The force created as the hot exhaust gases blast from the exhaust tube on a jet engine. Its power pushes the aircraft forward.

Top Gun Nickname for the Navy Fighter Weapons School. This is the graduate school for Navy fighter pilots at the Miramar Naval Air Station in San Diego, California. The term comes from old gunnery competitions held back in the 1950s.

Turbofan Jet engine with a large propellerlike fan that forces air into the engine. It also adds power by blowing air around the outside of a part of the engine called the compressor. The F-14 and A-10 are powered by turbofans.

The pilot cranks up the engines of his powerful F-14 Tomcat, waiting for the signal from the cat officer for a shot down the slippery flight deck.

Turbojet An older type of jet engine with a smaller fan that directs air through the engine but not around the outside. In the compressor, air is mixed with fuel and burned. Then it leaves as exhaust from the tail pipe. The F-4 and A-7 are turbojet-powered.

Two-holer Jet aircraft with two engines.

Universal pylons Fixtures located underneath the wings and fuselage of the plane. Called "universal" because almost all countries use the same design.

Variable-sweep wings Wings that can be moved forward and backward while the plane is in flight. When fully forward, the plane is slower, but able to turn easily. For maximum speed, the wings would be fully backward, as they would be while parked on a carrier deck.

VSTOL Vertical or Short Takeoff and Landing. The AV-8B Harrier Jump Jet is a VSTOL aircraft. It is able to take off vertically—heading straight up into the air—because of its unusual engine design.

WIZZO Air Force term for person in the back seat of a jet. It comes from Weapons System Officer. See "RIO."